Heirloom

poems by

Megan Krupa

Finishing Line Press
Georgetown, Kentucky

Heirloom

For Maren

Copyright © 2020 by Megan Krupa
ISBN 978-1-64662-361-7 First Edition
All rights reserved under International and Pan-American Copyright Conventions. No part of this book may be reproduced in any manner whatsoever without written permission from the publisher, except in the case of brief quotations embodied in critical articles and reviews.

ACKNOWLEDGMENTS

"Mountain Speak" first appeared in *Driftwood Press*
"Oral History" first appeared in the *Broad River Review* and was a finalist for the Ron Rash Award in Poetry, 2017 and for *Still: The Journal*'s Poetry Prize 2017
"Meditation on Interment" first appeared in *Cider Press Review*
"Defining X When X is (-1)" first appeared in *BOAAT*

Publisher: Leah Huete de Maines
Editor: Christen Kincaid
Cover Art: Matt Cohen
Author Photo: Michael Krupa
Cover Design: Elizabeth Maines McCleavy

Order online: www.finishinglinepress.com
also available on amazon.com

Author inquiries and mail orders:
Finishing Line Press
P. O. Box 1626
Georgetown, Kentucky 40324
U. S. A.

Table of Contents

Oral History 1

(The Child) Speak(s) to the Rhythm of Water 2

Open-Ended Burial 3

(The Child) Speak(s) (of a Sister) 4

Two Twelve Rising, and He Says He's Sorry 5

The (Polish) Wife Spells Her Goodbye in Refrigerator Magnets 6

The Will of Words 7

The Woman Speaks to the Rhythm of Water 9

If The Dirt Could Speak, ... 10

Defining X When X is (-1) 12

In My Sleep, I Speak the Language of Apology 13

Much in Waste, Much in Want 14

Meditation on Interment 15

Mountain History 16

When I Say I Am Angry 17

A Different Kind of Excavation 18

Eurydice Speaks Her Guilt 19

In My Dream, I See the Dead 20

The History of My Blood 21

Origin

Oral History

My grandfather would say
deceit was planted in the coalfield,
bound to the earth and hardened,
waiting for extraction,
to make new hands unclean.

That it spread its way into this family.
Leaving only toxic, black spittle
to settle in the cracks of our faces
when we smiled.

My grandmother would say
even the last breath of a life
isn't worth the acknowledgment of a first.

That if I had known to listen,
I might have heard a girl's name
in the spaces of her breathing.

Her name, soft,
like the way a small fist,
fingernails just beginning to bud,
latches onto the warmth of touch.

My cousin says
she doesn't like
driving past coalfields.

That she can never quite get
the grit out of her teeth.

(The Child) Speak(s) to the Rhythm of Water

She is lanky, in a sharp way
      that reminds me of edges,
falling vertical, narrow.

Her mouth opens slowly.
Like orange seeds surfacing,
making room
for words that are slippery, unfamiliar.

She is learning to talk her history.

Her hands used to tell the story,
signing her name with different letters
in a different order in a different town.

She is ageless in this discovery.

This life is predictable.

Like a series of breaths
moving in the same direction,
from the inside out.

Open-Ended Burial

When we lay them to the ground,
it is calmer.

No wonder people once believed the world was flat.
It's easier to understand a thing horizontally.

The incandescent glow
of a lie becoming truth becoming lie again
until it blooms into some unknowable object.

Like a sister (*breathe in*).
Like a family (*breathe out*).

A name you always knew
or a smell you can taste.

The memory becomes
mint-like and fragrant

until it takes you back to the time before

you can forget how
we all got our hands dirty.

(The Child) Speak(s) (of a Sister)

We're in a truck.

Ice-blue leather of the front seat and
the three of us piled high
on our way to Pennington Gap, Virginia.

Seven years old,
surrounded by frozen waterfalls,
and Papaw singing, "Frost on the Pumpkin."

I held my clear, plastic change purse,
multi-colored hearts,
in my hand, $2.50 in quarters,
and I knew this was my childhood.

Except there should have been four.

Each weekend we traveled to the land where people knew.

The town remembered my mother
coming to grieve for a summer
underneath laundry and elbow deep in garden dirt.

At 17, mourning the baby
handed over in a mint-green romper
to a woman who held the secrets of
our blood, and   she spilled them

until they took root in the soil.

Until burying one woman
upturned them all.

Two Twelve Rising, and He Says He's Sorry

Like he can categorize words.
Allowing one to outweigh
all the others spewing from his lips.

She decides to hold the words
in her mouth,
to tie them like a ribbon
with her teeth.

Her mother says,
it is the work of a woman,
she says,
the knot will hold.

The (Polish) Wife Spells Her Goodbye in Refrigerator Magnets

We've borrowed emotions that we cannot keep.

Sealed them in a glass box,
where their energy created a fog.

We could've traced our names in it,
if we could find the time it takes
to retrace anything anymore.

The Will of Words

I

Illness climbs onto her legs
like a transparent skin;
it settles gently, so as not to alarm

the doctors and nurses
who don't notice its hold.

II

Awake and feeling the weight of tomorrow,
the final meeting is scheduled.

There is nothing left to stand on anymore.

III

We watch the sunlight
melt into a strawberry sky.

When he texts me with the news,
all I can say is
it is the perfect night
for a reunion.

IV

Mourning is not passive.
It requires participation.
It requires ritual.
Like pouring a cup of coffee.
Like turning down the sheets before bed.

V

Her body is whole again,
if you can count the grains of ash
it would take to fill his hand.

The Woman Speaks to the Rhythm of Water

The rain hits hard
like the sound of fingernails
tapping, unforgivably loud,
an ignominious sound:
the sounds of flesh.

We've both been trying
to brea(the)k
for too many years.

Much like the night
you were in the front room
reimagining your life

while she was in the back room,
dying   is such art form.

Her fingernails turning
shades of cerulean and plum
marbleized against the porcelain
skin of my mother's hand.

Beginning and ending
with a sigh: the last sound
of human flesh,
the first breath of infinity.

If the Dirt Could Speak,

it would say spit back
my un(born)   lies
onto a blade of grass.

To bed, they go this time,
kneeling at the burial mound
I've made you.

Say her name,
whisper it once to me.

I can keep a secret.
I am light underfoot.

Reckoning

Defining X When X is (-1)

I needed to understand
the way air left her body.

If it was fast or slow.
If the lungs expanded.

I needed to know how much pressure
it took to relieve all the other pressures.

I can't say what I expected to find really.

A note, some mention of her,
buried web-deep, somewhere.

I want to know how a person
can lie on the living room floor
and not think about Christmas.

I need to know if the air was translucent.

If the popcorn ceiling
left purple lines when she closed her eyes.

Maybe they looked like dancers,
maybe they were comfort enough.

In My Sleep, I Speak the Language of Apology

It is like water, everywhere and connected.

You turn to face me.

Your palms are porcelain
always cold, a little like death.

It took seven years to grow a new skin
to replace the one I walked in at 19.

But even the first breath came from a loss.

Regeneration isn't easy,
Recuperation was slow.

Like learning to walk on two feet again
or learning to walk from the beginning.

It is a shame   it is easier
to craft language with our hands.

Your name has become broken letters.
Spilling out sideways and backward
until I rearrange them in my mouth.

Chewing between teeth and tongue.
Learning to speak again.
In a new tense: the present.

Now, when I say the name, Krupa,
I spit pieces of rib bone
out of my teeth.

Much in Waste, Much in Want

I've spent the majority of this life
ensuring I was the one left
       in this town the smokestacks whisper
their secrets to the darkness.

And only those of us, the early risers
will see their early morning conversations.

We are the keepers of the past lives.

At this hour everything has a promise,
a guaranteed ending of sorts.

But I am worn from the weight of it.

There was a girl who left once,
hands on her steering wheel.

I wonder if she said, "Eureka, I have found it."

When she stepped onto the coastland
we saw for the first time at 16.

Now, I imagine her body
footless, on birch leaves in a forest, somewhere.

What the weight
of an empty pocket must feel like
when you are lost and alone.

Meditation on Interment
For Krystal, on the day we buried your mother

Remember the time we buried
a goldfish in a film canister?

Copper-tinted tail folded,
tucked under the cap.

We laid her to rest in a flowerbed.

The deceased found bobbing
and limp only hours before,
with too little oxygen,
finally let go of breathing.

What did two little girls leave for the ground on that day?

A decaying goldfish,
eyes affixed and vacant,
splayed open for the world
to see its insides.

Mountain History

The electric-blue chill of the wind
makes its way around
hills, who have no knowledge of Spring

though it is March, and a steady unthawing
will soon rupture crystallized fragments.

Branches reach out to touch the sky,
at this height, we are the air now.

It is harder to breathe here.

Oxygen so thin it strangles,
leaving only the strong to rise up from the valley.

I buried myself here years ago,
stepped into the stubble-covered swells,

Into mahogany tinted dirt:
a chipped-stone pipe,
Tapir jaw bone,
the whisper of half-lives:
all beyond their own expirations.

And it is here I remain hidden.

The best of me pressed into the soil
the ground means more than
      the space it takes up.

When I Say I Am Angry,

I mean to say, I am sorry
for the loss of a child
for the loss of an identity
I never wanted but clung to in the end.

When I (don't) say a word,
I mean to say I am trying
to remember what it means to speak
in the language of the present.

Not the past
when the words connected
to form the sentences of my life
which I repeat to myself even now for comfort:

A little girl in a mint-green romper
held the hand of her mother,
she was an (only) child.
if only in her mind.

A Different Kind of Excavation

Around here they keep pulling bodies from the water.

Some washed up/ Some sought after/ Some discovered haphazardly years later by an unknown walker.

In Elizabethton, at Wilbur Dam,
a husband tried to save his own wife from drowning.

She went out too far.

Yesterday, my husband tried to save our goldfish.

It had been dying for two days at the bottom of our tank, drowning

> in
> too
> much
> water.

Its gills inflating the tiny torso.

We contemplated flushing it.

But even as I child, I knew to bury my dead.

Eurydice Speaks Her Guilt

I wring words from my lips
to tell the story of our love.

Pale, dull letters drip downward,
forming puddles at my feet.

They spell loss.
They spell mistake.

You were determined to recover
what was gone
what was taken—

while I was trapped
where even the light is afraid to show
her subtle whiteness.

But the graze of your touch,
too much for me now.

There was no bringing me
back when you turned to look,

I was gone.

In My Dream, I See the Dead

we buried resurface
to bear the weight of our feet.

I dream about a garden of goldfish.

Pale orange and gossamer,
the shape of peach slices.

They sprout up on stems.

They are no different from daisies
we plucked the petals off to predict
our future
(loves) won't know our future names.

We don't even know them ourselves.

I used to think I was an only child
until my sister appeared
diamond-like and real.

My family tried to bury her memory.

She unearthed herself.

The History of My Blood

Spills out slowly and crawls forward
to form letters and speak for itself.

The story of my happening,
of (t)he(i)rs
beginning with   an unk(no)wable thing.

How a mother/ gave away a daughter.
How a mother/ gave away a daughter.
How a mother/ gave away a daughter.

And I'm what's left.
I'm in the middle.

But now I carry my own,
and she has already inherited so much.

At night I cradle the full moon rising of my stomach.
Feel her stir and secretly fear I will lose her

as if I am unworthy to keep her
that the debt of our family must be paid.

The truth of it is
my family gave away three daughters.
Buried the story of their lives.
And tree-like I'm unable to trace my roots.

Notes

"The Woman Speaks to the Rhythm of Water "dying is such an art form is after Sylvia Plath and Elizabeth Bishop

Acknowledgments

I would like to take the opportunity to thank those publications that housed these poems first in various forms.

"Mountain Speak" first appeared in *Driftwood Press*

"Oral History" first appeared in the *Broad River Review* and was a finalist for the Ron Rash Award in Poetry, 2017 and for *Still: The Journal*'s Poetry Prize 2017

"Meditation on Interment" first appeared in *Cider Press Review*

"Defining X When X is (-1)" first appeared in *BOAAT*

I would like to extend my gratitude to the following:

The M.F.A. program at The University of Tampa. To my professors: Alan Michael Parker, Erica Dawson, and Donald Morrill, your advice and enthusiasm for our craft motivated me beyond measure.

My writing group, Elaine Riner, Rebecca Schamore, and Jon Tully, your insight and thoughtfulness was more than I could have asked. These poems are here because of you.
 Reese, Jerrod, Ian, Silk, and Margo, for the countless dinner conversations.

To the one who believed in me first, my writing teacher and friend, Timothy Davis.

To my family, for allowing me to tell our stories and supporting me through all the stages.

And to Michael, thank you for it all.

Megan Krupa's poetry has appeared in *BOAAT, Broad River Review,* and *Cider Press Review.* Her work was named a finalist for the Ron Rash Award in Poetry by *The Broad River Review* and for *Still: The Journal's* Poetry Prize. She has been named the Belz-Lipman Holocaust Educator of the year for the state of Tennessee and was a finalist for the Maya Angelou Teacher of Poetry Award given by the National Council of Teachers of English. Megan works as a poetry editor at Driftwood Press and teaches writing in Kingsport, Tennessee.

www.ingramcontent.com/pod-product-compliance
Lightning Source LLC
LaVergne TN
LVHW041519070426
835507LV00012B/1680